The Mediterranean Recipe for Everyone

The Health and Flavorful Mediterranean Cookbook with illustrated images for Beginners

Celine King

TABLE OF CONTENTS

Introduction

Examining the benefits of the Mediterranean diet requires us to dive deep into the foods that comprise it, as well as examine some significant research that has taken place over the years.

Understanding the science behind the diet is important because it helps you figure out how the diet works and, more importantly, the reasons behind the inclusion of certain food groups at the expense of others.

The Mediterranean diet isn't a magic formula, as I've mentioned. Its benefits are experienced over time, and this is when you'll realize the various health improvements. One of these benefits is the reduction of the risk of heart disease by over 22%, as indicated in a study conducted in 2018, which was published in JAMA Network Open (Gunnars, 2018).

Scientists posit that a number of smaller benefits of the diet add up to a sum that is much larger than its parts. The most significant advantage of the diet is the reduction of inflammation. In order to understand the various benefits the Mediterranean diet can offer, we need to understand what inflammation is and the health risks it poses.

Inflammation

Inflammation is actually a completely normal bodily function (Gunnars, 2018). Think of the last time you cut or wounded yourself. The area around the wound was tender, and the skin probably turned deep red in color. Soon, things were back to normal. This is a perfect example of the human immune system at its best.

Our body has the ability to heal itself and to even prevent a lot of diseases from manifesting in the first place. The immune system is how your body does this. This system is made up of an intricate network of organs and cells, and this isn't the kind of book that will delve deep into the various aspects of how it functions. Let's just say that it's a complex system and even seasoned scientists struggle to figure it out completely, as you'll shortly see.

The immune system springs into action the minute a threat to the body is detected. Let's say you cut yourself and draw blood. Your brain immediately sends a signal to the immune system, and its first step is to deploy the white cells present in your blood to start repairing the wound.

Our blood is comprised of two types of cells: white and red. Red blood cells carry oxygen and other important nutrients all around the body, while the white cells are the soldiers, so to speak. They aren't really white; the name signifies that their function is to protect rather than nourish. The minute a breach is detected, these cells begin fighting back against the virus or other bacteria that infect us. Once they've fought

these contaminants back, they get to work assisting in the creation of new tissue to replace the old one.

One of the signs the white blood cells look for prior to springing into action is inflammation. Biologically, inflammation is a complex chemical process, but for our purposes, you can think of it as being a signal beacon for your immune system to get active and remain active as long as the signal is on. Once your wound is healed, inflammation subsides, and your immune system calms back down.

As long as your immune system is active, your body is effectively at war. It prioritizes the healing process as much as possible and even hobbles you to a certain extent to stop you from doing further damage to yourself. For example, when your body is fighting a viral infection, it raises the temperature of your body, which stops you from functioning normally and forces you to rest. With you resting, there are fewer things for your body to take care of, and it can devote more resources to fighting the infection. What if the body fights the infection but doesn't succeed, though?

Breakfast

Stuffed Sweet Potato

Preparation time: 10 minutes

Cooking time: 40 minutes

Servings: 8

Ingredients:

- 8 sweet potatoes, pierced with a fork
- 14 ounces canned chickpeas, drained and rinsed
- 1 small red bell pepper, chopped
- 1 tablespoon lemon zest, grated
- 2 tablespoons lemon juice
- 3 tablespoons olive oil
- 1 teaspoon garlic, minced
- 1 tablespoon oregano, chopped
- 2 tablespoons parsley, chopped
- A pinch of salt and black pepper
- 1 avocado, peeled, pitted and mashed
- ¼ cup water
- ¼ cup tahini paste

Directions:

1. Arrange the potatoes on a baking sheet lined with parchment paper, bake them at 400 degrees F for 40 minutes, cool them down and cut a slit down the middle in each.
2. In a bowl, combine the chickpeas with the bell pepper, lemon zest, half of the lemon juice, half of the oil, half of the garlic, oregano, half of the parsley, salt and pepper, toss and stuff the potatoes with this mix.
3. In another bowl, mix the avocado with the water, tahini, the rest of the lemon juice, oil, garlic and parsley, whisk well and spread over the potatoes.
4. Serve cold for breakfast.

Nutrition: calories 308, fat 2, fiber 8, carbs 38, protein 7

Cauliflower Fritters

Preparation time: 10 minutes

Cooking time: 50 minutes

Servings: 4

Ingredients:

- o 30 ounces canned chickpeas, drained and rinsed
- o 2 and ½ tablespoons olive oil
- o 1 small yellow onion, chopped
- o 2 cups cauliflower florets chopped
- o 2 tablespoons garlic, minced
- o A pinch of salt and black pepper

Directions:

1. Spread half of the chickpeas on a baking sheet lined with parchment pepper, add 1 tablespoon oil, season with salt and pepper, toss and bake at 400 degrees F for 30 minutes.
2. Transfer the chickpeas to a food processor, pulse well and put the mix into a bowl.
3. Heat up a pan with the ½ tablespoon oil over medium-high heat, add the garlic and the onion and sauté for 3 minutes.
4. Add the cauliflower, cook for 6 minutes more, transfer this to a blender, add the rest of the chickpeas, pulse, pour over the crispy chickpeas mix from the bowl, stir and shape medium fritters out of this mix.
5. Heat up a pan with the rest of the oil over medium-high heat, add the fritters, cook them for 3 minutes on each side and serve for breakfast.

Nutrition: calories 333, fat 12.6, fiber 12.8, carbs 44.7, protein 13.6

Tuna Salad

Preparation time: 10 minutes

Cooking time: 0 minutes

Servings: 2

Ingredients:

- o 12 ounces canned tuna in water, drained and flaked
- o ¼ cup roasted red peppers, chopped
- o 2 tablespoons capers, drained
- o 8 kalamata olives, pitted and sliced
- o 2 tablespoons olive oil
- o 1 tablespoon parsley, chopped
- o 1 tablespoon lemon juice
- o A pinch of salt and black pepper

Directions:

1. In a bowl, combine the tuna with roasted peppers and the rest of the ingredients, toss, divide between plates and serve for breakfast.

Nutrition: Calories 250, Fat 17.3, Fiber 0.8, Carbs 2.7, Protein 10.1

Veggie Quiche

Preparation time: 6 minutes

Cooking time: 55 minutes

Servings: 8

Ingredients:

- ½ cup sun-dried tomatoes, chopped
- 1 prepared pie crust
- 2 tablespoons avocado oil
- 1 yellow onion, chopped
- 2 garlic cloves, minced
- 2 cups spinach, chopped
- 1 red bell pepper, chopped
- ¼ cup kalamata olives, pitted and sliced
- 1 teaspoon parsley flakes
- 1 teaspoon oregano, dried
- 1/3 cup feta cheese, crumbled
- 4 eggs, whisked
- 1 and ½ cups almond milk
- 1 cup cheddar cheese, shredded
- Salt and black pepper to the taste

Directions:

1. Heat up a pan with the oil over medium-high heat, add the garlic and onion and sauté for 3 minutes.
2. Add the bell pepper and sauté for 3 minutes more.
3. Add the olives, parsley, spinach, oregano, salt and pepper and cook everything for 5 minutes.
4. Add tomatoes and the cheese, toss and take off the heat.
5. Arrange the pie crust in a pie plate, pour the spinach and tomatoes mix inside and spread.
6. In a bowl, mix the eggs with salt, pepper, the milk and half of the cheese, whisk and pour over the mixture in the pie crust.
7. Sprinkle the remaining cheese on top and bake at 375 degrees F for 40 minutes.
8. Cool the quiche down, slice and serve for breakfast.

Nutrition: calories 211, fat 14.4, fiber 1.4, carbs 12.5, protein 8.6

Potato Hash

Preparation time: 10 minutes

Cooking time: 15 minutes

Servings: 4

Ingredients:

- A drizzle of olive oil
- 2 gold potatoes, cubed
- 2 garlic cloves, minced
- 1 yellow onion, chopped
- 1 cup canned chickpeas, drained
- Salt and black pepper to the taste
- 1 and ½ teaspoon allspice, ground
- 1 pound baby asparagus, trimmed and chopped
- 1 teaspoon sweet paprika
- 1 teaspoon oregano, dried
- 1 teaspoon coriander, ground
- 2 tomatoes, cubed
- 1 cup parsley, chopped
- ½ cup feta cheese, crumbled

Directions:

1. Heat up a pan with a drizzle of oil over medium-high heat, add the potatoes, onion, garlic, salt and pepper and cook for 7 minutes.
2. Add the rest of the ingredients except the tomatoes, parsley and the cheese, toss, cook for 7 more minutes and transfer to a bowl.
3. Add the remaining ingredients, toss and serve for breakfast.

Nutrition: calories 535, fat 20.8, fiber 6.6, carbs 34.5, protein 26.6

Leeks and Eggs Muffins

Preparation time: 10 minutes

Cooking time: 20 minutes

Servings: 2

Ingredients:

- o 3 eggs, whisked
- o ¼ cup baby spinach
- o 2 tablespoons leeks, chopped
- o 4 tablespoons parmesan, grated
- o 2 tablespoons almond milk
- o Cooking spray
- o 1 small red bell pepper, chopped
- o Salt and black pepper to the taste
- o 1 tomato, cubed
- o 2 tablespoons cheddar cheese, grated

Directions:

1. In a bowl, combine the eggs with the milk, salt, pepper and the rest of the ingredients except the cooking spray and whisk well.
2. Grease a muffin tin with the cooking spray and divide the eggs mixture in each muffin mould.
3. Bake at 380 degrees F for 20 minutes and serve them for breakfast.

Nutrition: calories 308, fat 19.4, fiber 1.7, carbs 8.7, protein 24.4

Artichokes and Cheese Omelet

Preparation time: 10 minutes

Cooking time: 8 minutes

Servings: 1

Ingredients:

- o   1 teaspoon avocado oil
- o   1 tablespoon almond milk
- o   2 eggs, whisked
- o   A pinch of salt and black pepper
- o   2 tablespoons tomato, cubed
- o   2 tablespoons kalamata olives, pitted and sliced
- o   1 artichoke heart, chopped
- o   1 tablespoon tomato sauce
- o   1 tablespoon feta cheese, crumbled

Directions:

1. In a bowl, combine the eggs with the milk, salt, pepper and the rest of the ingredients except the avocado oil and whisk well.
2. Heat up a pan with the avocado oil over medium-high heat, add the omelet mix, spread into the pan, cook for 4 minutes, flip, cook for 4 minutes more, transfer to a plate and serve.

Nutrition: calories 303, fat 17.7, fiber 9.9, carbs 21.9, protein 18.2

Quinoa and Eggs Salad

Preparation time: 5 minutes

Cooking time: 0 minutes

Servings: 4

Ingredients:

- 4 eggs, soft boiled, peeled and cut into wedges
- 2 cups baby arugula
- 2 cups cherry tomatoes, halved
- 1 cucumber, sliced
- 1 cup quinoa, cooked
- 1 cup almonds, chopped
- 1 avocado, peeled, pitted and sliced
- 1 tablespoon olive oil
- ½ cup mixed dill and mint, chopped
- A pinch of salt and black pepper
- Juice of 1 lemon

Directions:

1. In a large salad bowl, combine the eggs with the arugula and the rest of the ingredients, toss, divide between plates and serve for breakfast.

Nutrition: calories 519, fat 32.4, fiber 11, carbs 43.3, protein 19.1

Garbanzo Bean Salad

Preparation time: 10 minutes

Cooking time: 0 minutes

Servings: 4

Ingredients:

- 1 and ½ cups cucumber, cubed
- 15 ounces canned garbanzo beans, drained and rinsed
- 3 ounces black olives, pitted and sliced
- 1 tomato, chopped
- ¼ cup red onion, chopped
- 5 cups salad greens
- A pinch of salt and black pepper
- ½ cup feta cheese, crumbled
- 3 tablespoons olive oil
- 1 tablespoon lemon juice
- ¼ cup parsley, chopped

Directions:

1. In a salad bowl, combine the garbanzo beans with the cucumber, tomato and the rest of the ingredients except the cheese and toss.
2. Divide the mix into small bowls, sprinkle the cheese on top and serve for breakfast.

Nutrition: calories 268, fat 16, fiber 7, carbs 24, protein 9

Corn and Shrimp Salad

Preparation time: 10 minutes

Cooking time: 10 minutes

Servings: 4

Ingredients:

- o 4 ears of sweet corn, husked
- o 1 avocado, peeled, pitted and chopped
- o ½ cup basil, chopped
- o A pinch of salt and black pepper
- o 1 pound shrimp, peeled and deveined
- o 1 and ½ cups cherry tomatoes, halved
- o ¼ cup olive oil

Directions:

1. Put the corn in a pot, add water to cover, bring to a boil over medium heat, cook for 6 minutes, drain, cool down, cut corn from the cob and put it in a bowl.
2. Thread the shrimp onto skewers and brush with some of the oil.
3. Place the skewers on the preheated grill, cook over medium heat for 2 minutes on each side, remove from skewers and add over the corn.
4. Add the rest of the ingredients to the bowl, toss, divide between plates and serve for breakfast.

Nutrition: calories 371, fat 22, fiber 5, carbs 25, protein 23

Lunch Recipes

Rice and Fish Cakes

Preparation Time: 10 minutes

Cooking Time: 10 minutes

Servings: 6

Ingredients:

- o 6 oz salmon, canned, shredded
- o 1 egg, beaten
- o ¼ cup of basmati rice, cooked
- o 1 tsp. dried cilantro
- o ½ tsp. chili flakes
- o 1 tbsp. organic canola oil

Directions:

1. Mix salmon with egg, basmati rice, dried cilantro, and chili flakes.
2. Heat the organic canola oil in the skillet.
3. Make the small cakes from the salmon mixture and put in the hot oil.
4. Roast the cakes for 2 minutes per side or until they are light brown.

Nutrition: Calories: 123; Protein: 12.3g; Carbs: 7g; Fat: 6.3g

Salsa Rice

Preparation Time: 10 minutes

Cooking Time: 15 minutes

Servings: 6

Ingredients:

- o 9 oz long grain rice
- o 4 cups chicken stock
- o 1 cup of salsa
- o 2 tbsp. avocado oil

Directions:

1. Mix chicken stock and rice in the saucepan.
2. Cook the rice for 15 minutes on medium heat.
3. Then cool it to the room temperature and mix with avocado oil and salsa.

Nutrition: Calories: 109; Protein: 12.3g; Carbs: 7.4g; Fat: 6.3g

©pearlsa.com/blog

Seafood Rice

Preparation Time: 10 minutes

Cooking Time: 30 minutes

Servings: 4

Ingredients:

- ○ ½ cup seafood mix, frozen
- ○ ½ cup of long grain rice
- ○ 3 cups of water
- ○ 1 tbsp. olive oil
- ○ ½ tsp. ground coriander

Directions:

1. Boil the rice with water for 15-18 minutes or until it soaks all water.
2. Then heat olive oil in the saucepan.
3. Add seafood mix and ground coriander. Cook the ingredients for 10 minutes on low heat.
4. Then add rice, stir well, and cook for 5 minutes more.

Nutrition: Calories: 73; Protein: 12.3g; Carbs: 3.4g; Fat: 6.3g

Vegetarian Pilaf

Preparation Time: 10 minutes

Cooking Time: 30 minutes

Servings: 6

Ingredients:

- o   1 cup of long grain rice
- o   2 cups of water
- o   1 carrot, grated
- o   2 tbsp. olive oil
- o   1 tbsp. dried dill
- o   ½ tsp. dried mint
- o   ½ tsp. salt

Directions:

1. Boil rice with water for 15 minutes on medium heat.
2. Meanwhile, melt the olive oil and add the carrot.
3. Roast the carrot for 10 minutes or until it is soft.
4. Then add dried dill, mint, and cooked rice.
5. Carefully stir the pilaf and cook for 5 minutes.

Nutrition: Calories: 123; Protein: 10.3g; Carbs: 2.4g; Fat: 6.3g

Rice Rolls

Preparation Time: 15 minutes

Cooking Time: 35 minutes

Servings: 6

Ingredients:

- 4 white cabbage leaves
- 4 oz ground chicken
- ½ tsp. garlic powder
- ¼ cup of long grain rice, cooked
- ½ cup chicken stock
- ½ cup tomatoes, chopped

Directions:

1. In the bowl, mix ground chicken, garlic powder, and rice.
2. Then put the rice mixture on every cabbage leaf and roll.
3. Arrange the rice rolls in the saucepan.
4. Add chicken stock and tomatoes and close the lid.
5. Cook the rice rolls for 35 minutes on low heat.

Nutrition: Calories: 69; Protein: 12.3g; Carbs: 3.4g; Fat: 6.3g

Rice Stew with Squid

Preparation Time: 10 minutes

Cooking Time: 30 minutes

Servings: 6

Ingredients:

- o   5 oz long grain rice
- o   4 oz squid, sliced
- o   1 jalapeno pepper, chopped
- o   ½ cup tomatoes, chopped
- o   1 onion, diced
- o   2 cups chicken stock
- o   1 tbsp. avocado oil

Directions:

1.   Roast the onion with avocado oil in the skillet for 3-4 minutes or until the onion is light brown.
2.   Add squid, jalapeno pepper, and tomatoes.
3.   Cook the ingredients for 7 minutes.
4.   Then cook rice with water for 15 minutes.
5.   Add cooked rice in the squid mixture, stir, and cook for 3 minutes more.

Nutrition: Calories: 153; Protein: 12.3g; Carbs: 3.4g; Fat: 6.3g

Moroccan Lentil Soup

Preparation Time: 10 minutes

Cooking Time: 1 hour

Servings: 6

Ingredients:

- 2 tbsp. extra virgin olive oil
- 1 large yellow onion, finely chopped
- 2 stalks celery, finely chopped
- 1 carrot, peeled and finely chopped
- 1/3 cup chopped parsley, leaves and tender stems
- 1/2 cup chopped cilantro, leaves and tender stems
- 5 large garlic cloves, minced
- 2" piece ginger, minced
- 1 tsp. ground turmeric
- 1 tsp. ground cinnamon
- 2 tsp. sweet paprika
- 1/2 tsp. Aleppo pepper (or substitute freshly ground black pepper)
- 1 1/4 cups dry red lentils, rinsed and picked over
- 1 x 15 oz. can garbanzo beans, drained
- 1 x 28 oz. can sieved tomatoes
- 7–8 cups chicken broth or vegetable broth
- Coarse salt
- To Servings:
- Dates
- Lemon wedges

Directions:

1. Grab a large saucepan, add the olive oil and place over a medium heat.

2. Add the onion, celery, carrots, garlic, and ginger and cook for 5 minutes until soft.

3. Throw in the turmeric, cinnamon, paprika and pepper and continue to cook for another 5 minutes.

4. Add the tomatoes and broth, stir well then bring to a simmer.

5. Add the lentils, garbanzo beans, cilantro and parsley.

6. Cook uncovered for 35 minutes until the lentils become very soft.

7. Season well then serve and enjoy.

Nutrition: Calories: 551; Protein: 36.3g; Carbs: 33.4g; Fat: 30.3g

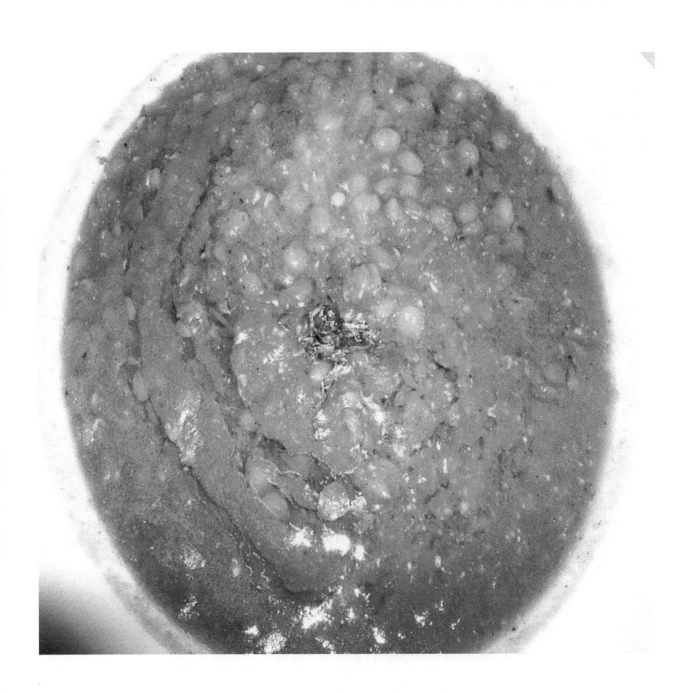

Roasted Red Pepper and Tomato Soup

Preparation Time: 10 minutes

Cooking Time: 45 minutes

Servings: 4

Ingredients:

- 2 red bell peppers, seeded and halved
- 3 tomatoes, cored and halved
- 1/2 medium onion, quartered
- 2 cloves garlic, peeled and halved
- 1-2 tbsp. olive oil
- 1/4 tsp. salt
- 1/4 tsp. ground black pepper
- 2 cups vegetable broth
- 2 tbsp. tomato paste
- 1/4 cup fresh parsley, chopped
- 1/4 tsp. Italian seasoning blend
- 1/4 tsp. ground paprika
- 1/8 teaspoon. ground cayenne pepper, or more to taste

Directions:

1. Preheat your oven to 375°F.
2. Grab a medium bowl and add the red peppers, tomatoes, onion, garlic, olive oil and salt and pepper. Toss well to coat.
3. Place onto a baking sheet and pop into the oven for 45 minutes until soft.
4. Next place the veggie broth over a medium heat and add the roasted veggies, tomato paste, parsley, paprika and cayenne.
5. Stir to combine then simmer for 10 minutes.
6. Use an immersion blender to puree the soup then return back to the pan.
7. Reheat if required, add extra seasoning then serve and enjoy.

Nutrition: Calories: 531; Protein: 26.3g; Carbs: 33.4g; Fat: 30.3g

Greek Spring Soup

Preparation Time: 10 minutes

Cooking Time: 35 minutes

Servings: 4

Ingredients:

- 6 cups chicken broth
- 1 1/2 cups diced or shredded cooked chicken
- 2 tbsp. olive oil
- 1 small onion, diced
- 1 bay leaf
- 1/3 cup arborio rice
- 1 large free-range egg
- 2 tbsp. water
- Juice of half of a lemon
- 1 cup chopped asparagus
- 1 cup diced carrots
- 1/2 cup fresh chopped dill, divided
- Salt and pepper, to tats

Directions:

1. Find a large pan, add the oil and place over a medium heat.
2. Add the onions and cook for five minutes until soft.
3. Next add ¼ cup dill, plus the chicken broth and bay leaf. Bring to a boil.
4. Add the rice and reduce the heat to low. Simmer for 10 minutes.
5. Add the carrots and asparagus and cook for 10 more minutes until the rice and veggies are tender.
6. Add the chicken and simmer.
7. Meanwhile find a medium bowl and add the egg, lemon and water. Whisk well.
8. Add ½ cup of the stock to the egg mixture, stirring constantly then pour it all back into the pot.
9. Heat through and allow the soup to thicken.
10. Add remaining dill, season well then serve and enjoy.

Nutrition: Calories: 551; Protein: 16.3g; Carbs: 23.4g; Fat: 10.3g

Fast Seafood Gumbo

Preparation Time: 10 minutes

Cooking Time: 40 minutes

Servings: 4

Ingredients:

- 1/4 cup olive oil
- 1/4 cup flour
- 1 medium white onion, chopped
- 1 cup celery, chopped
- 1 red or green bell pepper, chopped and deseeded
- 1 red chili, chopped
- 2 cups okra, chopped
- 1 cup canned crushed tomatoes
- 2 large cloves garlic, crushed
- 1 tsp. dried thyme
- 2 cups fish stock
- 1 bay leaf
- 1 tsp. cayenne powder
- 2 x 8 oz. can crab meat with brine
- 1 lb. shrimp, peeled and deveined
- Salt & pepper, to taste
- 1/4 cup fresh parsley, finely chopped

Directions:

1. Find a large pan, add the oil and place over a medium heat.
2. Add the flour and stir well until it forms a thick paste.
3. Add the onions, celery, peppers and okra and stir well, cooking for 5 minutes.
4. Add the garlic, tomatoes, thyme, stock, bay leaf and cayenne and stir again.
5. Bring to a boil then reduce the heat and simmer for 15 minutes.
6. Add the shrimp and crab and cook for 8 minutes more.

Nutrition: Calories: 551; Protein: 36.3g; Carbs: 33.4g; Fat: 30.3g

Dinner Recipes

Basmati Rice Pilaf Mix

Preparation Time: 10 minutes

Cooking Time: 15 minutes

Servings:

Ingredients:

- ¼ cup currants
- ¼ cup sliced almonds, toasted
- ¼ tsp. ground cinnamon
- ½ tsp. ground turmeric
- 1 small onion, chopped fine
- 1 tbsp. extra-virgin olive oil
- 1½ cups basmati rice, rinsed
- 2 garlic cloves, minced
- 2¼ cups water
- Salt and pepper

Directions:

1. Heat oil in a big saucepan on moderate heat until it starts to shimmer. Put in onion and ¼ tsp. salt and cook till they become tender, approximately five minutes. Put in rice, garlic, turmeric, and cinnamon and cook, stirring often, until grain edges begin to turn translucent, approximately three minutes.

2. Mix in water and bring to simmer. Decrease heat to low, cover, and simmer gently until rice becomes soft and water is absorbed, 16 to 18 minutes.

3. Remove from the heat, drizzle currants over pilaf. Cover, laying clean dish towel underneath lid, and let pilaf sit for about ten minutes. Put in almonds to pilaf and fluff gently with fork to combine. Sprinkle with salt and pepper to taste. Serve.

Nutrition: Calories: 234 Protein: 8 g Fat: 11 g Carbs: 33 g

Brown Rice Salad with Asparagus, Goat Cheese, and Lemon

Preparation Time: 10 minutes

Cooking Time: 15 minutes

Servings: 2

Ingredients:

- ¼ cup minced fresh parsley
- ¼ cup slivered almonds, toasted
- 1 lb. asparagus, trimmed and cut into 1-inch lengths
- 1 shallot, minced
- 1 tsp. grated lemon zest plus 3 tbsp. juice
- 1½ cups long-grain brown rice
- 2 oz. goat cheese, crumbled (½ cup)
- 3½ tbsp. extra-virgin olive oil
- Salt and pepper

Directions:

1. Bring 4 quarts water to boil in a Dutch oven. Put in rice and 1½ tsp. salt and cook, stirring intermittently, until rice is tender, about half an hour. Drain rice, spread onto rimmed baking sheet, and drizzle with 1 tbsp. lemon juice. Allow it to cool completely, about fifteen minutes.

2. Heat 1 tbsp. oil in 12-inch frying pan on high heat until just smoking. Put in asparagus, ¼ tsp. salt, and ¼ tsp. pepper and cook, stirring intermittently, until asparagus is browned and crisp-tender, about 4 minutes; move to plate and allow to cool slightly.

3. Beat remaining 2½ tbsp. oil, lemon zest and remaining 2 tbsp. juice, shallot, ½ tsp. salt, and ½ tsp. pepper together in a big container.

4. Put in rice, asparagus, 2 tbsp. goat cheese, 3 tbsp. almonds, and 3 tbsp. parsley. Gently toss to combine and allow to sit for about ten minutes. Sprinkle with salt and pepper to taste.

5. Move to serving platter and drizzle with remaining 2 tbsp. goat cheese, remaining 1 tbsp. almonds, and remaining 1 tbsp. parsley. Serve.

Nutrition: Calories: 242 Protein: 18 g Fat: 8 g Carbs: 12 g

Carrot-Almond-Bulgur Salad

Preparation Time: 10 minutes

Cooking Time: 20 minutes

Servings: 4

Ingredients:

- o   1/8 tsp. cayenne pepper
- o   1/3 cup chopped fresh cilantro
- o   1/3 cup chopped fresh mint
- o   1/3 cup extra-virgin olive oil
- o   ½ cup sliced almonds, toasted
- o   ½ tsp. ground cumin
- o   1 cup water
- o   1½ cups medium-grind bulgur, rinsed
- o   3 scallions, sliced thin
- o   4 carrots, peeled and shredded
- o   6 tbsp. lemon juice (2 lemons)
- o   Salt and pepper

Directions:

1. Mix bulgur, water, ¼ cup lemon juice, and ¼ tsp. salt in a container. Cover and allow to sit at room temperature until grains are softened and liquid is fully absorbed, about 1½ hours.

2. Beat remaining 2 tbsp. lemon juice, oil, cumin, cayenne, and ½ tsp. salt together in a big container.

3. Put in bulgur, carrots, scallions, almonds, mint, and cilantro and gently toss to combine. Sprinkle with salt and pepper to taste. Serve.

Nutrition: Calories: 287 Protein: 8 g Fat: 7 g Carbs: 13 g

Chickpea-Spinach Bulgur

Preparation Time: 5 minutes

Cooking Time: 20 minutes

Servings: 6

Ingredients:

- ¾ cup chicken or vegetable broth
- ¾ cup water
- 1 (15-oz.) can chickpeas, rinsed
- 1 cup medium-grind bulgur, rinsed
- 1 onion, chopped fine
- 1 tbsp. lemon juice
- 2 tbsp. zaatar
- 3 garlic cloves, minced
- 3 oz. (3 cups) baby spinach, chopped
- 3 tbsp. extra-virgin olive oil
- Salt and pepper

Directions:

1. Heat 2 tbsp. oil in a big saucepan on moderate heat until it starts to shimmer. Put in onion and ½ tsp. salt and cook till they become tender, approximately five minutes. Mix in garlic and 1 tbsp. zaatar and cook until aromatic, approximately half a minute.

2. Mix in bulgur, chickpeas, broth, and water and bring to simmer. Decrease heat to low, cover, and simmer gently until bulgur is tender, 16 to 18 minutes.

3. Remove from the heat, lay clean dish towel underneath lid and let bulgur sit for about ten minutes. Put in spinach, lemon juice, remaining 1 tbsp. zaatar, and residual 1 tbsp. oil and fluff gently with fork to combine. Sprinkle with salt and pepper to taste. Serve.

Nutrition: Calories: 234 Protein: 18 g Fat: 14 g Carbs: 10 g

Classic Baked Brown Rice

Preparation Time: 10 minutes

Cooking Time: 20 minutes

Servings: 6

Ingredients:

- o 1½ cups long-grain brown rice, rinsed
- o 2 tsp. extra-virgin olive oil
- o 2 1/3 cups boiling water
- o Salt and pepper

Directions:

1. Place the oven rack in the center of the oven and pre-heat your oven to 375°F. Mix boiling water, rice, oil, and ½ tsp. salt in 8-inch square baking dish.
2. Cover dish tightly using double layer of aluminum foil. Bake until rice becomes soft and water is absorbed, about 1 hour. Remove dish from oven, uncover, and gently fluff rice with fork, scraping up any rice that has stuck to bottom.
3. Cover dish with clean dish towel and let rice sit for about five minutes. Uncover and let rice sit for about five minutes longer.
4. Sprinkle with salt and pepper to taste. Serve.

Nutrition: Calories: 222 Protein: 18 g Fat: 10 g Carbs: 12 g

Preparation Time: 10 minutes

Cooking Time: 20 minutes

Servings: 4

Ingredients:

- 1/8 tsp. saffron threads, crumbled
- 1 (14.5-oz.) can diced tomatoes, drained
- 1 cup dry white wine
- 1 onion, chopped fine
- 1 tbsp. lemon juice
- 1 tsp. minced fresh thyme or ¼ tsp. dried
- 12 oz. large shrimp (26 to 30 per lb.), peeled and deveined, shells reserved
- 12 oz. small bay scallops
- 2 bay leaves
- 2 cups Arborio rice
- 2 cups chicken broth
- 2 tbsp. minced fresh parsley
- 2½ cups water
- 4 (8-oz.) bottles clam juice
- 5 garlic cloves, minced
- 5 tbsp. extra-virgin olive oil
- Salt and pepper

Directions:

1. Bring shrimp shells, broth, water, clam juice, tomatoes, and bay leaves to boil in a big saucepan on moderate to high heat.

2. Decrease the heat to a simmer and cook for 20 minutes. Strain mixture through fine-mesh strainer into big container, pressing on solids to extract as much liquid as possible; discard solids. Return broth to now-empty saucepan, cover, and keep warm on low heat.

3. Heat 2 tbsp. oil in a Dutch oven on moderate heat until it starts to shimmer. Put in onion and cook till they become tender, approximately five minutes.

4. Put in rice, garlic, thyme, and saffron and cook, stirring often, until grain edges begin to turn translucent, approximately three minutes.

5. Put in wine and cook, stirring often, until fully absorbed, approximately three minutes. Mix in 3½ cups warm broth, bring to simmer, and cook, stirring intermittently, until almost fully absorbed, about fifteen minutes.

6. Carry on cooking rice, stirring often and adding warm broth, 1 cup at a time, every few minutes as liquid is absorbed, until rice is creamy and cooked through but still somewhat firm in center, about fifteen minutes.

7. Mix in shrimp and scallops and cook, stirring often, until opaque throughout, approximately three minutes. Remove pot from heat, cover, and allow to sit for about five minutes.

8. Adjust consistency with remaining warm broth as required (you may have broth left over). Mix in remaining 3 tbsp. oil, parsley, and lemon juice and sprinkle with salt and pepper to taste. Serve.

Nutrition: Calories: 343 Protein: 18 g Fat: 14 g Carbs: 33 g

Classic Stovetop White Rice

Preparation Time: 10 minutes

Cooking Time: 10 minutes

Servings: 6

Ingredients:

- o   1 tbsp. extra-virgin olive oil
- o   2 cups long-grain white rice, rinsed
- o   3 cups water
- o   Basmati, jasmine, or Texmati rice can be substituted for the long-grain rice.
- o   Salt and pepper

Directions:

1. Heat oil in a big saucepan on moderate heat until it starts to shimmer. Put in rice and cook, stirring frequently, until grain edges begin to turn translucent, approximately two minutes.
2. Put in water and 1 tsp. salt and bring to simmer. Cover, decrease the heat to low, and simmer gently until rice becomes soft and water is absorbed, approximately twenty minutes.
3. Remove from the heat, lay clean dish towel underneath lid and let rice sit for about ten minutes. Gently fluff rice with fork. Sprinkle with salt and pepper to taste. Serve.

Nutrition: Calories: 252 Protein: 18 g Fat: 10 g Carbs: 33 g

Lamb and Chickpeas Stew

Preparation Time: 10 minutes

Cooking Time: 1 hour and 20 minutes

Servings: 6

Ingredients:

- 1 and ½ lb. lamb shoulder, cubed
- 3 tbsp. olive oil
- 1 cup yellow onion, chopped
- 1 cup carrots, cubed
- 1 cup celery, chopped
- 3 garlic cloves, minced
- 4 rosemary springs, chopped
- 2 cups chicken stock
- 1 cup tomato puree
- 15 oz. canned chickpeas, drained and rinsed
- 10 oz. baby spinach
- 2 tbsp. black olives, pitted and sliced
- A pinch of salt and black pepper

Directions:

1. Heat up a pot with the oil over medium-high heat, add the meat, salt and pepper and brown for 5 minutes.
2. Add carrots, celery, onion and garlic, stir and sauté for 5 minutes more.
3. Add the rosemary, stock, chickpeas and the other ingredients except the spinach and olives, stir and cook for 1 hour.
4. Add the rest of the ingredients, cook the stew over medium heat for 10 minutes more, divide into bowls and serve.

Nutrition: Calories 340, Fat 16gg, Fiber 3g, Carbs 21g, Protein 19g

Chorizo and Lentils Stew

Preparation Time: 10 minutes

Cooking Time: 35 minutes

Servings: 4

Ingredients:

- 4 cups water
- 1 cup carrots, sliced
- 1 yellow onion, chopped
- 1 tbsp. extra-virgin olive oil
- ¾ cup celery, chopped
- 1 and ½ tsp. garlic, minced
- 1 and ½ lb. gold potatoes, roughly chopped
- 7 oz. chorizo, cut in half lengthwise and thinly sliced
- 1 and ½ cup lentils
- ½ tsp. smoked paprika
- ½ tsp. oregano
- Salt and black pepper to taste
- 14 oz. canned tomatoes, chopped
- ½ cup cilantro, chopped

Directions:

1. Heat a saucepan with oil over medium high heat, add onion, garlic, celery and carrots, stir and cook for 4 minutes.
2. Add the chorizo, stir and cook for 1 minute more.
3. Add the rest of the ingredients except the cilantro, stir, bring to a boil, reduce heat to medium-low and simmer for 25 minutes.
4. Divide the stew into bowls and serve with the cilantro sprinkled on top. Enjoy!

Nutrition: Calories 400, Fat 16gg, Fiber 13g, Carbs 58g, Protein 24g

Lamb and Potato Stew

Preparation Time: 10 minutes

Cooking Time: 2 hours

Servings: 4

Ingredients:

- 2 and ½ lb. lamb shoulder, boneless and cut in small pieces
- Salt and black pepper to taste
- 1 yellow onion, chopped
- 3 tbsp. extra virgin olive oil
- 3 tomatoes, grated
- 1 and ½ cups chicken stock
- ½ cup dry white wine
- 1 bay leaf
- 2 and ½ lb. gold potatoes, cut into medium cubes
- ¾ cup green olives

Directions:

1. Heat a saucepan with the oil over medium high heat, add the lamb, brown for 10 minutes, transfer to a platter and keep warm for now.
2. Heat the pan again, add onion, stir and cook for 4 minutes.
3. Add tomatoes, stir, reduce heat to low and cook for 15 minutes.
4. Return lamb meat to pan, add wine and the rest of the ingredients except the potatoes and olives, stir, increase heat to medium high, bring to a boil, reduce heat again, cover pan and simmer for 30 minutes.
5. Add potatoes and olives, stir, cook for 1 more hour., divide into bowls and serve.

Nutrition: Calories 450, Fat 12gg, Fiber 4g, Carbs 33g, Protein 39g

Snacks

Rosemary Cauliflower Dip

Preparation Time: 10 minutes

Cooking Time: 15 minutes

Servings: 4

INGREDIENTS

- 1 lb. cauliflower florets
- 1 tbsp fresh parsley, chopped
- 1/2 cup heavy cream
- 1/2 cup vegetable stock
- 1 tbsp garlic, minced
- 1 tbsp rosemary, chopped
- 1 tbsp olive oil
- 1 onion, chopped
- Pepper
- Salt

DIRECTIONS

1. Add oil into the inner pot of instant pot and set the pot on sauté mode.
2. Add onion and sauté for 5 minutes.
3. Add remaining ingredients except for parsley and heavy cream and stir well.
4. Seal pot with lid and cook on high for 10 minutes.
5. Once done, allow to release pressure naturally for 10 minutes then release remaining using quick release. Remove lid.
6. Add cream and stir well. Blend cauliflower mixture using immersion blender until smooth.
7. Garnish with parsley and serve.

NUTRITION: Calories 128 Fat 9.4 g Carbohydrates 10.4 g Sugar 4 g Protein 3.1 g Cholesterol 21 mg

Tomato Olive Salsa

Preparation Time: 10 minutes

Cooking Time: 5 minutes

Servings: 4

INGREDIENTS

- o   2 cups olives, pitted and chopped
- o   1/4 cup fresh parsley, chopped
- o   1/4 cup fresh basil, chopped
- o   2 tbsp green onion, chopped
- o   1 cup grape tomatoes, halved
- o   1 tbsp olive oil
- o   1 tbsp vinegar
- o   Pepper
- o   Salt

DIRECTIONS

1.   Add all ingredients into the inner pot of instant pot and stir well.
2.   Seal pot with lid and cook on high for 5 minutes.
3.   Once done, allow to release pressure naturally for 5 minutes then release remaining using quick release. Remove lid.
4.   Stir well and serve.

NUTRITION: Calories 119 Fat 10.8 g Carbohydrates 6.5 g Sugar 1.3 g Protein 1.2 g Cholesterol 0 mg

Easy Tomato Dip

Preparation Time: 10 minutes

Cooking Time: 13 minutes

Servings: 4

INGREDIENTS

- o   2 cups tomato puree
- o   1/2 tsp ground cumin
- o   1 tsp garlic, minced
- o   1/4 cup vinegar
- o   1 onion, chopped
- o   1 tbsp olive oil
- o   Pepper
- o   Salt

DIRECTIONS

1.   Add oil into the inner pot of instant pot and set the pot on sauté mode.
2.   Add onion and sauté for 3 minutes.
3.   Add remaining ingredients and stir well.
4.   Seal pot with lid and cook on high for 10 minutes.
5.   Once done, allow to release pressure naturally for 10 minutes then release remaining using quick release. Remove lid.
6.   Blend tomato mixture using an immersion blender until smooth.
7.   Serve and enjoy.

NUTRITION: Calories 94 Fat 3.9 g Carbohydrates 14.3 g Sugar 7.3 g Protein 2.5 g Cholesterol 0 mg

Balsamic Bell Pepper Salsa

Preparation Time: 10 minutes

Cooking Time: 6 minutes

Servings: 2

INGREDIENTS

- o 2 red bell peppers, chopped and seeds removed
- o 1 cup grape tomatoes, halved
- o 1/2 tbsp cayenne
- o 1 tbsp balsamic vinegar
- o 2 cup vegetable broth
- o 1/2 cup sour cream
- o 1/2 tsp garlic powder
- o 1/2 onion, chopped
- o Salt

DIRECTIONS

1. Add all ingredients except cream into the instant pot and stir well.
2. Seal pot with lid and cook on high for 6 minutes.
3. Once done, release pressure using quick release. Remove lid.
4. Add sour cream and stir well.
5. Blend the salsa mixture using an immersion blender until smooth.
6. Serve and enjoy.

NUTRITION: Calories 235 Fat 14.2 g Carbohydrates 19.8 g Sugar 10.7 g Protein 9.2 g Cholesterol 25 mg

Spicy Chicken Dip

Preparation Time: 10 minutes

Cooking Time: 15 minutes

Servings: 10

INGREDIENTS

- o 1 lb. chicken breast, skinless and boneless
- o 1/2 cup sour cream
- o 8 oz cheddar cheese, shredded
- o 1/2 cup chicken stock
- o 2 jalapeno pepper, sliced
- o 8 oz cream cheese
- o Pepper
- o Salt

DIRECTIONS

1. Add chicken, stock, jalapenos, and cream cheese into the instant pot.
2. Seal pot with lid and cook on high for 12 minutes.
3. Once done, release pressure using quick release. Remove lid.
4. Shred chicken using a fork.
5. Set pot on sauté mode. Add remaining ingredients and stir well and cook until cheese is melted.
6. Serve and enjoy.

NUTRITION: Calories 248 Fat 19 g Carbohydrates 1.6 g Sugar 0.3 g Protein 17.4 g Cholesterol 83 mg

Slow Cooked Cheesy Artichoke Dip

Preparation Time: 10 minutes

Cooking Time: 60 minutes

Servings: 6

INGREDIENTS

- o   10 oz can artichoke hearts, drained and chopped
- o   4 cups spinach, chopped
- o   8 oz cream cheese
- o   3 tbsp sour cream
- o   1/4 cup mayonnaise
- o   3/4 cup mozzarella cheese, shredded
- o   1/4 cup parmesan cheese, grated
- o   3 garlic cloves, minced
- o   1/2 tsp dried parsley
- o   Pepper
- o   Salt

DIRECTIONS

1. Add all ingredients into the inner pot of instant pot and stir well.
2. Seal the pot with the lid and select slow cook mode and set the timer for 60 minutes. Stir once while cooking.
3. Serve and enjoy.

NUTRITION: Calories 226 Fat 19.3 g Carbohydrates 7.5 g Sugar 1.2 g Protein 6.8 g Cholesterol 51 mg

Olive Eggplant Spread

Preparation Time: 10 minutes

Cooking Time: 8 minutes

Servings: 12

INGREDIENTS

- o 1 3/4 lbs. eggplant, chopped
- o 1/2 tbsp dried oregano
- o 1/4 cup olives, pitted and chopped
- o 1 tbsp tahini
- o 1/4 cup fresh lime juice
- o 1/2 cup water
- o 2 garlic cloves
- o 1/4 cup olive oil
- o Salt

DIRECTIONS

1. Add oil into the inner pot of instant pot and set the pot on sauté mode.
2. Add eggplant and cook for 3-5 minutes. Turn off sauté mode.
3. Add water and salt and stir well.
4. Seal pot with lid and cook on high for 3 minutes.
5. Once done, release pressure using quick release. Remove lid.
6. Drain eggplant well and transfer into the food processor.
7. Add remaining ingredients into the food processor and process until smooth.
8. Serve and enjoy.

NUTRITION: Calories 65 Fat 5.3 g Carbohydrates 4.7 g Sugar 2 g Protein 0.9 g Cholesterol 0 mg

Pepper Tomato Eggplant Spread

Preparation Time: 10 minutes

Cooking Time: 10 minutes

Servings: 3

INGREDIENTS

- o 2 cups eggplant, chopped
- o 1/4 cup vegetable broth
- o 2 tbsp tomato paste
- o 1/4 cup sun-dried tomatoes, minced
- o 1 cup bell pepper, chopped
- o 1 tsp garlic, minced
- o 1 cup onion, chopped
- o 3 tbsp olive oil
- o Salt

DIRECTIONS

1. Add oil into the inner pot of instant pot and set the pot on sauté mode.
2. Add onion and sauté for 3 minutes.
3. Add eggplant, bell pepper, and garlic and sauté for 2 minutes.
4. Add remaining ingredients and stir well.
5. Seal pot with lid and cook on high for 5 minutes.
6. Once done, release pressure using quick release. Remove lid.
7. Lightly mash the eggplant mixture using a potato masher.
8. Stir well and serve.

NUTRITION: Calories 178 Fat 14.4 g Carbohydrates 12.8 g Sugar 7 g Protein 2.4 g Cholesterol 0 mg

Healthy Coconut Blueberry Balls

Preparation Time: 10 minutes

Cooking Time: 10 minutes

Servings: 12

Ingredients:

- ¼ cup flaked coconut
- ¼ cup blueberries
- ½ tsp. vanilla
- ¼ cup honey
- ½ cup creamy almond butter
- ¼ tsp. cinnamon
- 1 ½ tbsp. chia seeds
- ¼ cup flaxseed meal
- 1 cup rolled oats, gluten-free

Directions:

1. In a large bowl, add oats, cinnamon, chia seeds, and flaxseed meal and mix well.
2. Add almond butter in microwave-safe bowl and microwave for 30 seconds. Stir until smooth.
3. Add vanilla and honey in melted almond butter and stir well.
4. Pour almond butter mixture over oat mixture and stir to combine.
5. Add coconut and blueberries and stir well.
6. Make small balls from oat mixture and place onto the baking tray and place in the refrigerator for 1 hour.
7. Serve and enjoy.

Nutrition: Calories 129, Fat 7.4g, Carbs 14.1g, Sugar 7g, Protein 4 g, Cholesterol 0 mg

Crunchy Roasted Chickpeas

Preparation Time: 10 minutes

Cooking Time: 25 minutes

Servings: 4

Ingredients:

- 15 oz can chickpeas, drained, rinsed and pat dry
- ¼ tsp. paprika
- 1 tbsp. olive oil
- ¼ tsp. pepper
- Pinch of salt

Directions:

1. Preheat the oven to 450°F.
2. Spray a baking tray with cooking spray and set aside.
3. In a large bowl, toss chickpeas with olive oil and spread chickpeas onto the prepared baking tray.
4. Roast chickpeas in preheated oven for 25 minutes. Shake after every 10 minutes.
5. Once chickpeas are done then immediately toss with paprika, pepper, and salt.
6. Serve and enjoy.

Nutrition: Calories 157, Fat 4.7g, Carbs 24.2g, Protein 5.3g,

Tasty Zucchini Chips

Preparation Time: 10 minutes

Cooking Time: 15 minutes

Servings: 8

Ingredients:

- 2 medium zucchini, sliced 4mm thick
- ½ tsp. paprika
- ¼ tsp. garlic powder
- ¾ cup parmesan cheese, grated
- 4 tbsp. olive oil
- ¼ tsp. pepper
- Pinch of salt

Directions:

1. Preheat the oven to 375°F.
2. Spray a baking tray with cooking spray and set aside.
3. In a bowl, combine the oil, garlic powder, paprika, pepper, and salt.
4. Add sliced zucchini and toss to coat.
5. Arrange zucchini slices onto the prepared baking tray and sprinkle grated cheese on top.
6. Bake in preheated oven for 15 minutes or until lightly golden brown.
7. Serve and enjoy.

Nutrition: Calories 110, Fat 9.8g, Carbs 2.2g, Protein 4.4g

Dessert Recipes

Crunchy Sesame Cookies

Preparation Time: 10 minutes

Cooking Time: 15 minutes

Servings: 14-16

INGREDIENTS:

- o 1 cup sesame seeds, hulled
- o 1 cup sugar
- o 8 tablespoons (1 stick) salted butter, softened
- o 2 large eggs
- o 1¼ cups flour

DIRECTIONS:

1. Preheat the oven to 350°F. Toast the sesame seeds on a baking sheet for 3 minutes. Set aside and let cool.

2. Using a mixer, cream together the sugar and butter. Put the eggs one at a time until well-blended. Add the flour and toasted sesame seeds and mix until well-blended.

3. Drop spoonful of cookie dough onto a baking sheet and form them into round balls, about 1-inch in diameter, similar to a walnut.

4. Put in the oven and bake for 5 to 7 minutes or until golden brown. Let the cookies cool and enjoy.

NUTRITION: Calories 218 Fat 12g Carbs 25g Protein 4g

Mini Orange Tarts

Preparation Time: 45 minutes

Cooking Time: 0 minutes

Servings: 2

INGREDIENTS

- o   1 cup coconut flour
- o   1/2 cup almond flour
- o   A pinch of grated nutmeg
- o   A pinch of sea salt
- o   1/4 teaspoon ground cloves
- o   1/4 teaspoon ground anise
- o   1 cup brown sugar
- o   6 eggs
- o   2 cups heavy cream
- o   2 oranges, peeled and sliced

DIRECTIONS

1. Begin by preheating your oven to 350 degrees F.
2. Thoroughly combine the flour with spices. Stir in the sugar, eggs, and heavy cream. Mix again to combine well.
3. Divide the batter into six lightly greased ramekins.
4. Top with the oranges and bake in the preheated oven for about 40 minutes until the clafoutis is just set. Bon appétit!

NUTRITION: Calories: 398; Fat: 28.5g; Carbs: 24.9g; Protein: 11.9g

Traditional Kalo Prama

Preparation Time: 45 minutes

Cooking Time: 0 minutes

Servings: 2

INGREDIENTS

- 2 large eggs
- 1/2 cup Greek yogurt
- 1/2 cup coconut oil
- 1/2 cup sugar
- 8 ounces semolina
- 1 teaspoon baking soda
- 2 tablespoons walnuts, chopped
- 1/4 teaspoon ground nutmeg
- 1/4 teaspoon ground anise
- 1/2 teaspoon ground cinnamon
- 1 cup water
- 1 ½ cups caster sugar
- 1 teaspoon lemon zest
- 1 teaspoon lemon juice

DIRECTIONS

1. Thoroughly combine the eggs, yogurt, coconut oil, and sugar. Add in the semolina, baking soda, walnuts, nutmeg, anise, and cinnamon.

2. Let it rest for 1 ½ hour.

3. Bake in the preheated oven at 350 degrees F for approximately 40 minutes or until a tester inserted in the center of the cake comes out dry and clean.

4. Transfer to a wire rack to cool completely before slicing.

5. Meanwhile, bring the water and caster sugar to a full boil; add in the lemon zest and lemon juice, and turn the heat to a simmer; let it simmer for about 8 minutes or until the sauce has thickened slightly.

6. Cut the cake into diamonds and pour the syrup over the top; allow it to soak for about 2 hours. Bon appétit!

NUTRITION: Calories: 478; Fat: 22.5g; Carbs: 62.4g; Protein: 8.2g

Turkish-Style Chocolate Halva

Preparation Time: 20 minutes

Cooking Time: 0 minutes

Servings: 2

INGREDIENTS

- 1/2 cup water
- 2 cups sugar
- 2 cups tahini
- 1/4 teaspoon cardamom
- 1/4 teaspoon cinnamon
- A pinch of sea salt
- 6 ounces dark chocolate, broken into chunks

DIRECTIONS

1. Bring the water to a full boil in a small saucepan. Add in the sugar and stir. Let it cook, stirring occasionally, until a candy thermometer registers 250 degrees F. Heat off.

2. Stir in the tahini. Continue to stir with a wooden spoon just until halva comes together in a smooth mass; do not overmix your halva.

3. Add in the cardamom, cinnamon, and salt; stir again to combine well. Now, scrape your halva into a parchment-lined square pan.

4. Microwave the chocolate until melted; pour the melted chocolate over your halva and smooth the top.

5. Let it cool to room temperature; cover tightly with a plastic wrap and place in your refrigerator for at least 2 hours. Bon appétit!

NUTRITION: Calories: 388; Fat: 27.5g; Carbs: 31.6g; Protein: 7.9g

Rice Pudding with Dried Figs

Preparation Time: 45 minutes

Cooking Time: 0 minutes

Servings: 2

INGREDIENTS

- o 3 cups milk
- o 1 cup water
- o 2 tablespoons sugar
- o 1/3 cup white rice, rinsed
- o 1 tablespoon honey
- o 4 dried figs, chopped
- o 1/2 teaspoon cinnamon
- o 1/2 teaspoon rose water

DIRECTIONS

1. In a deep saucepan, bring the milk, water and sugar to a boil until the sugar has dissolved.
2. Stir in the rice, honey, figs, raisins, cinnamon, and turn the heat to a simmer; let it simmer for about 40 minutes, stirring periodically to prevent your pudding from sticking.
3. Afterwards, stir in the rose water. Divide the pudding between individual bowls and serve. Bon appétit!

NUTRITION: Calories: 228; Fat: 6.1g; Carbs: 35.1g; Protein: 7.1g

Conclusion

The Mediterranean diet is not a short program packed with hours of exercise and slight, flavorless meals that have no taste nor keep the hunger pangs away. The diet is a way of life, a completely different way of thinking, and a unique way of approaching diets than what has been sold to all those desperate to shed the pounds.

There's no need to count calories when you adopt the Mediterranean diet. I'm sure if calories were a subject in school, we'd all have doctorates in it by now. With a glass of wine, say goodbye to unhealthy fats and hello to healthy fats.

Olives and nuts, which have been shown to encourage longevity and improve health, contain good kinds of fat.

When you go grocery shopping, the frozen food aisle will no longer be your first stop. The more seasonal—sensational—the fresher, the better.

You still don't have to say goodbye to bread, which is good news. Unfortunately, white bread is no longer an option. Most western diets will prioritize bread and carbohydrates as elements to be eliminated. Whole-grain slices of bread, on the other hand, are there to be enjoyed—in moderation, of course, but sufficiently in the diet to not want, need, or lack it.

Another marvelous revelation that comes with this way of eating is that the variety of foods that you can eat are endless. Your menu can change from week to week and is versatile enough to switch out ingredients for others without hampering the flavors and tastes.

Because the Mediterranean is so diverse, foods from countries such as Italy, France, Morocco, Spain, Turkey, and Greece can be explored. There is plenty of room to get creative in the kitchen—and, as all good Mediterranean do, include your family and friends.

Just as the cuisine is varied, so is the list of herbs and spices that you can include when whipping up something delicious. Herbs and spices are a fundamental part of living in the Mediterranean. Many of the herbs are also rich in minerals and nutrients, meaning it would be wise to stock up on them.

In all honesty, simple is the way to go, even when preparing food. Remaining true to your ingredients and keeping them as unrefined as possible are a few fundamentals. We all live busy lives, and it is hard to want to come home and still have to think about a meal—let alone a healthy one—to make for the family and yourself. Cooking in the Mediterranean way is less complex, choosing to keep the produce as close to unrefined as possible. How well does a mezze platter sound with a glass of wine? There's your dinner conundrum solved for one evening, and it ticks all the right boxes when it comes to the diet.

This is a lifestyle, a way in which to truly embrace a new way of eating, exercising, and living. It is about achieving equilibrium in what we put into our bodies and how to stay happy.

You will never feel hungry, and that is guaranteed—most, if not all of the foods allow your body to digest them slowly, meaning you will stay fuller for longer.

This brings me to my final point. All of the above sounds too good to be true, but it is not—best of all, eating this way really can help you lose weight. Feeling content and satisfied in life leaves you less room to stray, as conventional diets do. Lastly, your heart will thank you, as all the foods on the list support its function and will keep it beating steadily along.

Though it may seem so, the Mediterranean diet is not new to us. This diet is more about tradition if you think about it. It's a look back at how we used to live when we were younger, or maybe how our parents did when they were children. There were no hurried meals in front of televisions—plates were piled high with the freshest foods, food was shared by family members at dining room tables, and people were present, eager to share their day with those they cared for.

As you have read through this book, you should have found that you were given all sorts of information about the Mediterranean diet. Whether you are new to dieting, simply looking for a change, or you just thought that the food sounded good, switching to a Mediterranean diet is great for you. It can really help you boost your own general wellness while emphasizing the importance of a healthy lifestyle. You will nourish not only your body but also your mind and your heart when you make use of this lifestyle, and in return, you will be healthier. You will feel better. You will feel happier. You may even live longer!

At the end of the day, all you have to do is make sure that you follow those main principles. Pay attention to what you are eating on a regular basis. Make sure that the food that you are eating is wholesome and healthy. Ensure that you spend time with your family and eat meals with your loved ones. Always get some daily exercise into your life so you know that you are keeping your body in the best condition that you can. If you can do this, you will find that life is easier than ever. You will feel better than ever. You will find that you are healthier than ever, and all you had to do was change the way that you looked at food.

Finally, if this book has succeeded in teaching you everything that you could need to know and you feel like you did get that benefit out of this book, please consider heading over to Amazon to leave behind a review. Your feedback and opinion are always greatly appreciated!

Indulge in a glass of wine. In addition to raising your HDL (the "healthy" cholesterol), and preserving your coronary arteries, drinking wine in moderation will reduce your chances of developing cardiovascular diseases. Several research studies have shown that the right amounts of wine consumption— one glass (5 oz) or less per day— have its benefits. Wine helps dilate the arteries and increase blood flow within your body. Wine phenols also aid in reducing bad cholesterol. When you drink alcohol, try drinking one 5-ounce glass of wine per day.

Eat smaller portions. The portions that are usually served in the US are much greater than required. Large portions, when consumed, can lead to weight gain, excess calorie intake, and obesity.

Measure portions of all groceries. To stay on track, you can use a food scale or weigh cups. Guessing or "eye-balling" portions usually results in larger portions than is required.

Exercise regularly. People are far more involved in the countries bordering the Mediterranean than in the

US. Their increased level of activity is partly the reason why they consider their lifestyle very healthy. Physical activity has been associated with many health benefits, including increased levels of high-density lipoprotein (HDL or "healthy" cholesterol), decreased levels of triglycerides, decreased risk of diabetes and high blood pressure, enhanced arthritis-related pain, and decreased cancer rates. Seek to do aerobic exercise of moderate intensity at least for 30 minutes during each session five days a week. This will help you meet the US minimum physical activity requirement of 150 minutes per week. Take up walking, running, cycling, swimming, and hiking to get aerobic exercise. Include two to three days of 20-minute strength training every week. You should also try Pilates or yoga that will help build your strength and flexibility. Walk and move more throughout the day. People living in the Mediterranean are taking part in more leisure practices compared to people living in the US. It has been shown that being more active over the day has similar benefits to aerobic activity. Lifestyle practice is the activity that you embed in your daily routine. Taking the stairs, for example, or mopping down the concrete, are called lifestyle behaviors. Throughout their day's Mediterranean people tend to have more activity in the lifestyle. For instance, we're cycling to and from destinations or riding a bike instead. Involvement is an essential part of your daily routine. Think of your day, the schedule for your work, and the whole week. Where can you put in more movement or more steps? Can you ride a motorcycle to work? Can you go to the drugstore or grocery store? Should you take the stairs instead of the lift? Try to incorporate more moves into your day.

Eat mindfully. Another feature of a Mediterranean diet and lifestyle is that they usually eat more carefully compared to the American hustle and bustle. Conscious eating can help you eat less, enjoy eating more, and even help you lose weight. It's a way to eat carefully. It's a way to eat that makes you more aware of what kind of food you consume, how much you eat, and how easily you eat.

Manage stress. Chronic lifestyle stress can be tough to deal with. Studies have shown, however, that people living in Mediterranean countries can deal with stress better and suffer less from heart disease. Try to tackle as much tension as possible. Try to listen to music, exercise, meditate, do yoga, or converse with a friend or family member. When stress management is too complicated, see a life coach or therapist for additional assistance.

Thank you for taking this book with you as your guide to the Mediterranean diet. Hopefully, as you read through this book, you found that this diet was as compelling to you as it has been to millions of others. Hopefully, you feel confident enough in yourself, your knowledge, and what you would need to do to ensure that you can properly make an informed decision on the content of this book. Hopefully, as you head off into the world, you are able to make use of this diet, the benefits that it offers, and you will enjoy it.

Lightning Source UK Ltd.
Milton Keynes UK
UKHW050824170521
383853UK00002B/7